Boone

GLE 2.8
AR NO Quiz

What Pets Teach Us

Willow Creek Press
Minocqua, Wisconsin

Published by Willow Creek Press
P.O. Box 147
Minocqua, Wisconsin 54548

Editor/Design: Andrea Donner

Printed in Canada

Eat plenty of **fruits...**

...and vegetables every day.

A few **treats** are okay too…

…but too many can
make your **belly** hurt.

Smile!

Someone
is sure to
smile
back.

Get plenty of **exercise** every day…

…and lots
of **rest** after
playing.

Learning
to **read**
is **fun**
for you and
your friends.

Be **curious** about the world around you.

There's a lot to **learn!**

If you **listen** when someone is talking to you...

…they'll listen to you when you are talking to them!

Be careful when
you explore new places…

... and ask for **help** if you get into **trouble**.

Keep **looking** if you can't find something.

Everybody
needs to
take a
bath.

It's not
always easy,
but you
should
share
what you
have with
others.

If you make a **mess**,
clean up after yourself.

Home is the place that is **safe** and **warm** and **cozy**.

If someone is **picking** on you…

...**ignore** them and swim away.

It's **cool** to have friends…

...so don't be **afraid**

to make **new** ones.

Some **friends** don't
look anything like you…

...but they can **still** be
friends just the same.

Hug a **friend**
if they're
feeling **sad**...

...and **ask** your parents if
they can come over to **play**.

All friends and pets and people
should be **respected.**

Even little ones!

Guess what?
You are very
special.

There is **no one** else just like **you!**